City Safari

Hedgehog

Hampsh
Te

Isabel Thomas

Raintree is an imprint of Capstone Global Library Limited, a company incorporated in England and Wales having its registered office at 7 Pilgrim Street, London, EC4V 6LB – Registered company number: 6695582

www.raintreepublishers.co.uk
myorders@raintreepublishers.co.uk

Text © Capstone Global Library Limited 2014
First published in hardback in 2014
Paperback edition first published in 2015
The moral rights of the proprietor have been asserted.

Edited by Dan Nunn, Rebecca Rissman, and Helen Cox Cannons
Designed by Tim Bond
Original illustrations © Capstone Global Library Ltd 2014
Picture research by Mica Brancic
Production by Helen McCreath
Originated by Capstone Global Library Ltd
Printed and bound in China

ISBN 978 1 406 27130 0 (hardback)
17 16 15 14 13
10 9 8 7 6 5 4 3 2 1

ISBN 978 1 406 27137 9 (paperback)
18 17 16 15
10 9 8 7 6 5 4 3 2

British Library Cataloguing in Publication Data
A full catalogue record for this book is available from the British Library.

Acknowledgements
We would like to thank the following for permission to reproduce photographs: Alamy pp. 10 (© Les Stocker), 14 (© blickwinkel/Hecker); FLPA pp. 4 (Minden Pictures/Konrad Wothe), 6 (Paul Hobson), 7 (Imagebroker/Kurt Kracher), 8 (Foto Natura Stock), 11 (Minden Pictures/Ingo Arndt), 12 (Foto Natura Stock), 13 (Paul Hobson), 15 (Roger Tidman), 19 (Paul Hobson), 23 hibernate (Minden Pictures/Ingo Arndt); Getty Images p. 9 inset (BSIP/UIG); Naturepl.com p. 9 main (© David Tipling), 15 (© Chris O'Reilly), 17 (© Dave Bevan Photography), 18 (© David Heuclin), 20, 21 & 23 (all © Jane Burton); Shutterstock pp. 5 (© CreativeNature.nl), 16 (© Lena Lir), 23 senses (© CreativeNature.nl), 23 pesticide (© Kasia Bialasiewicz); 23 nocturnal (© Philipp1983).
Front cover photograph of a hedgehog reproduced with permission of Shutterstock © PRILL); background Shutterstock (© LilKar); back cover reproduced with permission of Shutterstock (© Lena Lir).

We would like to thank Michael Bright for his invaluable help in the preparation of this book.

Every effort has been made to contact copyright holders of material reproduced in this book. Any omissions will be rectified in subsequent printings if notice is given to the publisher.

Warning!

Never touch wild animals or their homes. Some wild animals carry diseases. Scared animals may bite or scratch you. If you find a sick or injured hedgehog, tell an adult. Advice on how to help a sick or injured hedgehog can be found on the websites listed on page 24.

Note about spotter icon

Your eyes, ears, and nose can tell you if a hedgehog is nearby. Look for these clues as you read the book, and find out more on page 22.

spines

hairy belly

snout

claws

They live in busy towns and cities, too.

Come on a city safari. Find out if hedgehogs are living near you.

Why do hedgehogs live in towns and cities?

Countryside hedgehogs live near woodlands and hedgerows.

This is where they find shelter, food, and water.

Hedgehogs can find everything they need in towns and cities, too.

Gardens, churchyards, and parks are full of things to eat and places to hide.

What makes hedgehogs good at living in towns and cities?

Being small and shy helps hedgehogs to live near people.

They can climb walls and squeeze through holes to go where they want to.

A good **sense** of smell helps hedgehogs to find food.

They can also sniff out danger, and climb, swim, or run to safety.

Where do hedgehogs hide?

Hedgehogs are **nocturnal**. This means they rest during the day.

They hide in long grass, under plants, or in nests made of leaves and twigs.

Each hedgehog has lots of different hiding places.

In winter, hedgehogs build an extra-safe and warm nest in which to **hibernate**.

What do hedgehogs eat?

For most of the year, hedgehogs come out every night to look for food.

They catch earthworms, beetles, earwigs, and caterpillars.

3

Hedgehogs also eat slugs and snails, but they try to wipe the slime off first.

Birds' eggs and dead animals are special treats.

Why do hedgehogs like living near people?

City hedgehogs do not have to wander far to find food and drink.

Gardens are full of bird food, pet food, and thrown-away scraps.

Some people even leave out water and special hedgehog food.

Small, finger-shaped droppings show that a hedgehog has visited.

What dangers do hedgehogs face in towns and cities?

When a hedgehog is frightened, it rolls up into a ball.

Its sharp spines may stop a fox or badger from eating it.

Sadly, a hedgehog's spines cannot protect it from human-made dangers.

Cars kill many thousands of hedgehogs every year.

How can people help hedgehogs?

Don't drop litter! This will stop hedgehogs getting stuck inside empty bottles or pots.

Adults should check for hedgehogs before cutting grass, or burning wood and leaves.

Gardeners can avoid using **pesticides** that poison hedgehogs.

Some people build nest boxes to keep hedgehogs safe while they **hibernate**.

Do hedgehogs always live alone?

Hedgehogs eat, rest, and sleep alone for most of the year.

If male and female hedgehogs meet in the spring, they often **mate**.

A month later, the female has up to seven babies, called **hoglets**.

She looks after them until they are old enough to live in the city without her.

Hedgehog spotter's guide

Look back at the sights, sounds, and smells that tell you a hedgehog might be nearby. Use these clues to go on your own city safari.

1 Hedgehogs leave small footprints with five toe marks.

2 Summer nests can be hard to spot. They look like piles of sticks and leaves.

3 Hedgehogs are noisy eaters. They make loud crunching noises when eating beetles, and slobbery, sucking noises when eating worms and slugs! They also huff and puff when moving around.

4 Look for finger-shaped hedgehog droppings on lawns. They may sparkle with tiny pieces of beetle shell!

Picture glossary

 **hibernate** spend the winter in a deep sleep

 **mate** when a male and female animal get together to have babies

 **nocturnal** active mostly at night

 **pesticide** poisons that kill pests (animals that do damage), such as rats and slugs

 **sense** find out what is around through sight, hearing, smell, taste, and touch

Find out more

Books

The RHS Wildlife Garden, Martyn Cox (Dorling Kindersley, 2009)

Wild Town, Mike Dilger (A & C Black, 2012)

Websites

www.britishhedgehogs.org.uk
Learn all about hedgehogs and how to help protect them on this website.

www.hedgehogstreet.org
Become a hedgehog champion! Learn more on this website.

Index